We Have Marched Together

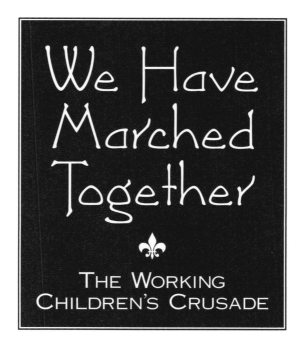

We Have Marched Together

THE WORKING CHILDREN'S CRUSADE

STEPHEN CURRIE

LERNER PUBLICATIONS COMPANY • MINNEAPOLIS

Front cover: Addie Laird (top image), a spinner in a cotton mill, told adults who asked that she was 12 years old. Other girls in the mill said she was really 10.

Page 2: A young boy works at the Cheney Silk Mills, in Manchester, Connecticut.

Library of Congress Cataloging-in-Publication Data

Currie, Stephen, 1960–
    We have marched together : the working children's crusade / Stephen Currie.
        p.   cm.
    Includes bibliographical references and index.
    Summary: Examines the problem of child labor during the early twentieth century, focusing on a protest march from Philadelphia to New York City in 1903 by a group of child textile workers led by Mother Jones.
    ISBN 0-8225-1733-7 (alk. paper)
    1. Children—Employment—Pennsylvania—Philadelphia—History—Juvenile literature. 2. Textile workers—Pennsylvania—Philadelphia—History—Juvenile literature. 3. Kensington (Philadelphia, Pa.)—Juvenile literature. 4. Demonstrations—United States—History—Juvenile literature. 5. Jones, Mother, 1843?–1930—Juvenile literature. [1. Children—Employment—History. 2. Jones, Mother, 1843?–1930.] I. Title.
HD6247.T42U63   1997
331.3'1'097309041—dc20   95-47686

Manufactured in the United States of America
1 2 3 4 5 6 – JR – 02 01 00 99 98 97

Contents

TO WORK

Oh! Isn't it a pity
that such a pretty girl as I
Should be sent to the factory
to pine away and die?

> —Sung by workers,
> Lowell, Massachusetts, 1837

They seemed impossibly tiny to be working, but each morning they headed off to jobs in factories, sweatshops, and mills. They were the child workers of Philadelphia in the early 1900s.

One of these workers was William Hartley. The son of a carpet weaver, William was born in 1892. He followed in his father's footsteps. William attended school only to age 8. By the time he was 13, he was working "full time" in Dobson's Mills, one of Philadelphia's largest textile factories. Over and over again, six days a week, William put two of his fingers on a spool of yarn and twisted it. For four years at Dobson's, that was his job.

William wasn't at all unusual. At that time, thousands of children across the United States worked long days in places like Dobson's Mills.

Often they earned only pennies per hour. Nowhere was the problem more severe than in Philadelphia. When Philadelphia's children marched off to work each morning, they looked like a miniature army. A labor reformer estimated that Philadelphia had more children at work than New York City; more than the entire states of Ohio and Illinois; and enough, if all the children stood side by side, to "form a line reaching from the doors of the city hall far beyond the city limits on the west."

Gus Misuinas made cotton stockings at the Tommy Brown Hosiery Factory in Philadelphia. He was 12 years old and earned $2.50 a week helping to run a machine. "I worked from seven to six P.M.," Gus remembered, "and on Saturdays from seven to two P.M. I didn't like it. The hours were too long." Gus's working days *were* long. Counting a few short lunch breaks, Gus was in the factory for 62 hours each week.

By 1903, children such as this boy could be found in almost any mill. In some factories, children were already working by the age of six.

Girls had similar experiences. In 1902, 12-year-old Catherine Hutt went to work at a knitting mill. Her working hours were "from 6:30 in the morning until six at night"—even longer than Gus's. At age 14, Catherine switched to working in a paper mill. "All I did," she said years later, describing her job, "was fold the ends of each roll as they came out." How did she enjoy the work? About as much as Gus enjoyed his job: "I hated it."

"THE ENDLESS ROWS OF SPINDLES"

William, Gus, and Catherine—before she moved on to the paper mill—all worked in the textile industry, which included many different kinds of jobs and factories. Some textile workers spun cotton fibers into thread. Others did the same work with silk. Still others wove the threads into cloth. "Fine-grain" mills produced expensive, decorative cloth. "Coarse-grain" factories churned out material that was much cheaper and less fancy. There were mills that produced stockings, mills that manufactured shirts, and mills that made nothing but rugs. All were textile mills.

Philadelphia's first textile factories had been built before 1820. By 1903, the city was a center of textile manufacturing. According to one count, there were about 800 different textile companies in Philadelphia, and 100 more in towns nearby. No industry brought more money to Philadelphia or employed more workers—children as well as adults.

We don't know exactly how many children were employed by textile makers in Philadelphia in the early 1900s. Estimates for the year 1900, for instance, range from 6,000 to almost four times that number. At a very minimum, more than 10 percent of all Philadelphia textile workers were under 16, and many observers said that figure was far too low.

Children were concentrated in the lowest-paying jobs. In stocking factories like the one where Gus Misuinas worked, one out of every five workers was a child. There were also many children in knitting and spinning mills where coarse, less expensive cloth was produced. The work these children did was dull and repetitive. Usually they tended automatic knitting machines and replaced spools of thread.

The textile industry was especially important to a community called Kensington, in the northeastern part of Philadelphia. Settled mostly by immigrants from Ireland and England, Kensington grew quickly once the mills came to town. By 1900, just about half of all Philadelphia textile mills operated in Kensington. Almost a quarter of a million people—including William, Gus, and Catherine—called the neighborhood home.

In textile mills, the young workers were often dwarfed by the machinery. Here boys and girls take a break from work to pose for a photographer.

When the mills were running, Kensington residents young and old worked hard. During the 1880s and 1890s, mill employees averaged more than 60 hours of work a week. Even national holidays didn't necessarily mean time off for workers. The owners of John Gay's Sons, a carpet factory in Philadelphia, kept detailed records about their business. "Thanksgiving Day," read their logbook. "Mill will stop at noon."

Still, hard work did not translate into good pay and working conditions. Even adults rarely earned over 15 cents an hour; many children took home much less. The smaller children often had to crawl beneath heavy power looms, oilcan in hand, lubricating the metal pieces as the machines ran full blast. If the children were injured, and they often were, they could lose their jobs. Workers were at the mercy of their employers, too. The owners of Dobson's Mills sometimes fired workers just for carrying matches in their pockets. Smoking on the premises was forbidden, and the owners simply assumed that any worker with matches was planning to smoke sometime before leaving for the day. When orders fell, factories would lay off workers or cut their pay, and there wasn't much the workers could do about it. No matter how low wages got, or how terrible the working conditions might be, the mills could always find someone else in need of a job.

THE WORKERS OF KENSINGTON

Since so many textile mills were in Kensington, that neighborhood was home to most of Philadelphia's textile workers, too. But Kensington was not an easy place in which to live. Though many mill families owned their own houses, the buildings tended to be cramped and run-down. Philadelphia has often been associated with culture and learning; Kensington didn't have much of either. Instead of libraries, churches, and museums, Kensington was famous for its bars. "Within an area of five square blocks," one witness reported, "there were one hundred and thirty-five saloons." Schools in the neighborhood rarely went past the elementary grades. But few children in Kensington seriously considered staying in school longer.

A view of Kensington in 1905, taken from the Bromley Carpet Mills

Most Kensington families needed the extra money that working children could provide. According to many estimates, families couldn't earn enough money to support themselves even if both parents worked in the mill full-time. Given a choice between sending a child to work or to school, most poor families picked the factory. Indeed, for many, there was never any choice. "Two and two may be four," one reformer wrote, "but the baby has no milk, the child has no shoes, and the house is cold, even when he has figured and read and written for a month."

Much of the blame for child labor lay with the mill owners. Quite simply, child laborers were usually a better bargain than adults. Not only could they be paid less—often less than half what an adult would demand for comparable work—but many young teenagers could actually do better work than their parents. A few mill jobs could only be done by young children with nimble fingers and small, quick bodies. Most textile mills gave jobs to entire families, not individuals. In fact, it was almost impossible for an adult to get a textile job without putting children in the family to work, too.

But mill owners were not the only ones who liked the system the way it was. Some parents who could afford to send their children to school still didn't. They preferred to spend their children's earnings. A Massachusetts mill boy, Frederick Brown, was sent to the mill partly so his aunt and uncle, who served as his guardians, could buy more liquor.

In Kensington, those mothers who did not work in the mills often did piecework at home. Children helped out as soon as they were able.

In New York, a girl named Fannie Harris told officials that she worked so her mother wouldn't have to. Asked if she could spell the word *cat,* Fannie replied "Yes, sir." Asked, "How do you spell it?" Fannie answered "I have forgot."

Schools were not helpful, either. Teachers had little patience with poor children, disruptive kids, and children who didn't speak English well. Most schools got rid of these kids as soon as they could. In Chicago, a factory inspector found thousands of 10- and 11-year-olds who had been expelled from school. The only alternative, for most, was the factory. In Massachusetts, schools set up two tracks: a regular curriculum and a "mill school" for those who were expected to leave soon for the factory. For mill children, education was considered virtually useless. As Fannie Harris demonstrated, the students learned very little.

Besides parents, schools, and mill owners, however, there was another group that liked the system. Surprisingly enough, many child workers were delighted to be going into the mills, especially at first. When still in school, Frederick Brown liked to tease the younger students: "Don't you wish YOU could go into the mills in a few months and earn money like WE'RE going to do, eh?" Working meant earning money, even if only a little, and money meant independence. When he started work, Frederick's aunt and uncle treated him like royalty for a few days.

Other young mill workers agreed with Frederick. One reformer asked 500 child laborers if they would prefer to go to work or go to school, assuming they had enough money to do either. Less than a hundred chose school. "The boss don't never hit me," one boy explained. At school, he said, "they hits ye if ye don't learn, and they hits ye if ye whisper, and they hits ye if ye have string in yer pocket."

ORGANIZED LABOR

Few Philadelphians thought much about working children or the problems they faced. So many children across the United States had jobs, most observers thought it was nothing out of the ordinary. Indeed, it was expected that a child from a poor family—a Catherine Hutt or a

Mill workers young and old dressed for safety. Short skirts, rolled-up sleeves, and tight braids all protected working girls from becoming caught in machinery.

William Hartley—would leave school early and be employed full-time by age 12 or so. As a result, when people tried to change the system, they worked on behalf of all workers, not just children.

By the 1890s, many Philadelphia textile workers had banded together into labor unions to make things better. When workers formed a union, they could bargain collectively; that is, they could negotiate their hours and wages together rather than one by one. Unions varied in size from many thousands of members down to only a few hundred, but they all gave workers more power than they would otherwise have had. If conditions were not to the liking of a union, its members sometimes went on strike and simply refused to work until they got what they wanted. That cost owners money, but not every strike was successful. Especially during small strikes that affected only one or two unions, mills often hired replacement workers to keep production going. The owners called these nonunion workers "strikebreakers;" the strikers called them "scabs."

Philadelphia's textile mills had serious labor problems during the last part of the 1800s. It seemed as though some union was always on strike against some factory. In 1886 alone, there were almost 100 different strikes. Some unions struck on a regular basis. One worker at Dobson's Mills remembered walking out "every time the blue birds came out in summer." Not all strikes were over serious issues. As a young teenager, one textile worker used to start strikes at her factory for no particular reason. "It was boring, you know," she reported years later. "We just wanted to see some excitement." But when union members struck over real problems, they argued their cases well. Whether about money, hours, or working conditions, the strikes were usually settled in the workers' favor.

Shortly after 1900, however, the balance of power began to shift. In the late 1880s, some of the owners of the biggest mills had gotten together and formed a group called the Philadelphia Manufacturers' Association. At first, this association tried to influence national politics. The owners pushed for laws that would make their businesses more profitable and easier to run. But after a few years, the owners realized that their group could also be a powerful weapon against strikers. Just as workers could unionize and present a united front, so too could mill owners work together to defeat a strike.

"WE WANT TIME TO PLAY"

In 1903, the owners' association was put to the test. In a show of strength, representatives from 39 different unions met and agreed to push toward a single goal: reducing textile workers' hours from 60 to 55 a week. It was the first time that so many textile unions had tried to work together. Before 1903, most labor disputes had been limited to just a few unions or only a handful of factories. This demand was different.

Members of the Philadelphia Manufacturers' Association met at their club to discuss strategy during the mill strike of 1903.

The proposal from these unions would affect nearly every textile worker—including children—and nearly every textile mill in the city of Philadelphia.

In April, the combined unions took their demands to the manufacturers. Union leaders did not expect the owners to agree without a fight. They were right. According to the John Gay's Sons logbook, several rug mill owners met at the Manufacturers' Club, where they played cards and pledged "to resist the unjust demands and methods of their employees." One factory owner argued that Philadelphia workers already had better working conditions than they deserved, especially compared to textile workers elsewhere in the country. A manufacturers' journal called the workers' requests "unreasonable and exorbitant." "It is an utter impossibility," a columnist wrote, "to comply with these demands."

So many rug and carpet mills were located along Second Street and Allegheny Avenue in Kensington that the area was nicknamed Carpet Row.

But mill owners didn't stop there. Secretly, the manufacturers' association asked all of its members to pay a forfeit, a kind of fine. For every loom in a factory, the mill owner had to pay $20. For a 100-loom factory, then, the forfeit came to $2,000—quite a lot of money! Forfeits were added for other equipment, too. If the unions went on strike, the association members would hold the forfeits until the strike was over.

As this ad for a dyeing company shows, Kensington textile mills had many different specialties.

Factories that met the unions' demands would lose their forfeits to the other members of the association. That was a strong incentive not to cave in to the workers, and most members of the association agreed to participate.

Privately, however, a handful of mill owners admitted that the workers were not being so unreasonable, after all. One mill owner who refused to pay a forfeit argued that new machinery made it possible for his workers to do as much in 55 hours as they used to in 60. Another mill owner, James Pollock, agreed that "there is some justice" in the demand, but he insisted that the owners stand firm anyway. If they didn't, Pollock wrote in a newspaper column, "the manufacturers will shortly be 'held up' again with renewed claims and demands."

The unions knew nothing about the forfeits. When their request for fewer hours was rejected, they began to plan a strike. The targeted date was June 1. On that day, they warned manufacturers, textile workers all over Philadelphia would walk away from their spindles, their looms, and their dyeing tubs—unless their demands were met.

The manufacturers refused to budge. On Saturday, May 30, John Gay's Sons posted this notice on their front door:

> In reply to the request of the Employees of this Establishment for a reduction of working hours from 60 to 55 per week, we feel compelled to decline this request.
>   This mill will be open as usual on Monday morning, June 1st, at 6:30 o'clock.

But on Monday, no employees showed up at John Gay's Sons. Of the 63 rug companies in Philadelphia, 62 were shut down. In less than a week, 7 of every 10 textile workers had left their jobs.

The strike was on.

STRIKE!

Little children shall not toil,
Under or above the soil,
In the good time coming.
  —Charles Mackay,
  "The Good Time Coming"

The strike of 1903 brought a welcome vacation for many of the working children of Kensington and other Philadelphia neighborhoods. Away from the roar of knitting machines, girls like Catherine Hutt could hope to hear birds singing. Without the need to stand and twist spools all day, children like William Hartley could play a game of baseball on an empty lot. And all textile workers would have a chance to catch up on needed sleep, a precious commodity. Child workers, in particular, sometimes came home so exhausted that they refused to spend their days off playing with friends. Sleep, as one young worker told her mother, was "lots more fun."

No one wanted the strike to last too long, however. With no wages coming in, families would have trouble paying rent and buying food. If Kensington residents ever needed to stick together, the strike of 1903 was the time. A few small mills gave in to the strikers' requests right away, but the rest refused to budge. To make any gains at all, the workers would have to hold firm in their demands. Yet even as the strike began, the workers were already showing signs of disagreement.

DIVISIONS IN THE RANKS

The biggest question was money. Going from 60 hours to 55 meant less time on the job, and less time on the job seemed likely to lower most workers' wages. For many strikers, this was not a big concern. The best-paid workers, all of them adults, were willing to sacrifice a little money for some extra free time. Plenty of other textile workers were paid "by the piece," or according to how much they produced during the day. Some of them expected to earn the same amount of money just by working a little harder, or by using improved machinery. Thirty-six of the 39 unions that called the strike agreed not to demand higher wages.

Some workers, however, felt that they could not risk getting paid less. This was especially true among the lowest-paid strikers, as well as among workers who were paid by the hour. The wool spinners' union voted to hold out for the same amount of pay as before. Two other unions demanded a pay increase to go along with fewer hours. Three unions may not sound like much, but these three were among the biggest in all Philadelphia. Together, they represented about one textile worker out of every six, including most of the mill children. So, when the strikers should have been concentrating on opposing management, they were arguing among themselves.

The strikers also could not agree on strategy. During most earlier Philadelphia textile strikes, workers had been out on the streets marching and singing songs of protest. Day after day, union leaders had talked to reporters about their demands. Every chance they got, strikers had insulted the mill owners. Many strike veterans felt that these were the tactics to use in 1903, as well. But most strike leaders disagreed. As a result, the 1903 strike began calmly and politely. There was no name-calling, no loud protest marches, and no chanting union members picketing outside the mills.

As the strike moved into its second week, the mill owners continued to work together. Members of the manufacturers' association met regularly to talk about the strikers' demands. The owners were willing to be patient. John Gay's Sons canceled its orders, recalled its entire sales force, and settled down to wait out the workers. Charles Doak, who helped run a spinning mill, actually welcomed the strike. It gave him a chance to fix looms and give the factory a thorough cleaning. "There are a great many things," he said, "that can be seen and need attending to when the machinery is stopped." Few owners seemed eager to make any concessions at all. Indeed, most manufacturers would not even discuss the unions' demands with the workers.

By the third week of the strike, the textile workers were growing concerned. So far, their plans hadn't worked. To convince the manufacturers to negotiate, the workers needed a leader who could grab the attention of the mill owners, the newspapers, and the public. No one in the local unions had that kind of charisma. So the workers brought in their secret weapon: labor organizer "Mother" Mary Jones.

"THE GOOD MOTHER"

No labor leader in the United States was as beloved by workers as Mother Jones. We don't know exactly how old she was at the time of the Philadelphia strike, but most estimates place her somewhere between 60 and 75. Mother Jones had been involved in labor disputes since the 1880s. A small, white-haired woman who usually wore the same simple dress each day, she was an effective and tireless worker. Most of her time was spent organizing coal miners in Pennsylvania, West Virginia, and Colorado. However, Jones was willing to help workers anywhere she was needed. She had no permanent home. Instead, she crisscrossed the country from one strike to another, living with workers and encouraging them to stick together no matter what. Whether helping out miners, railroad workers, or factory employees, Mother Jones always won her "children's" respect and admiration.

But Mother Jones wasn't just determined. She was also flamboyant.

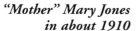
"Mother" Mary Jones
in about 1910

A compelling speaker, Mother Jones was rarely polite when she talked about the owners of factories and mines. "Dictators," "tyrants," and "cannibals" were some of the nicer names she used to describe them. Moreover, Mother Jones would do whatever it took to help her people. To learn about conditions in textile mills, she hadn't just talked to textile workers. Instead, she hid her true identity and worked in several Southern factories to experience the workers' problems firsthand.

Mother Jones had a good sense of the dramatic, too. Once she was forbidden to enter a mining village, so she disguised herself as a peddler and walked in without anyone giving her a second glance. Another time, she armed miners' wives with mops and brooms and led them in an attack on strikebreakers. When she was arrested, which was often, she made sure there was a reporter nearby to cover the story.

Mother Jones's supporters felt just as strongly about her as her enemies did. Here the wives of striking Colorado miners march in support of Jones, who was imprisoned at the time.

On June 14, Mother Jones arrived in Philadelphia. Right away, she began to stir things up. She traveled around the city, calling the textile strike just one battle of a "great industrial war." The fight, she said, was between the workers and the "capitalists," or rich mill owners, and Jones never let anyone forget whose side she was on. In speech after speech, she promised to keep the fight going "until the last capitalist shall surrender." The mill owners, she told strikers, "tell you they cannot afford to give you shorter hours. But who built those big mills?" If the manufacturers were really out of money, she added sarcastically, "I tell you what to do, start up a soup-house for them tomorrow." That was the kind of talk the strike had been missing, and Mother Jones provided plenty of it.

Just as they were supposed to, Mother Jones's words irritated the mill owners. A few of them couldn't help talking back. Several insisted fiercely that Jones did not represent *their* employees. "Not one in ten of our people wanted to go out" on strike, one manufacturer told the press, implying that Jones and the other leaders had intimidated workers into following their call for a strike. With some manufacturers growing nervous, Robert Dornan, a rug maker, reassured owners that Mother Jones would not be successful. "There is no justice in the present strike, and it is bound to fail," he wrote, "Mother Jones and the other agitators of such ilk to the contrary."

Jones did more than just insult the owners. After every speech, she collected money to share among the strikers. She also spent a lot of time trying to convince the strikers to cooperate, focusing on the three unions that wanted more pay. Afraid that they might destroy the strike with their extra demands, Jones put pressure on them to fight for fewer hours first, more pay later. "You shouldn't come out with any demand for wages," she told them. "There is time enough for everything." But her words were unsuccessful. The men and women who belonged to these unions refused to change their minds.

"THE MOST HEART-RENDING SPECTACLE"

The strikers that Mother Jones noticed most of all were neither men nor women. They were children. Arriving in the city, she saw children mixed in among the adult strikers, children impossibly small to be working in the mills. "How old are you?" she would ask. And they would reply, "I am just a little over ten, Mother." Some were even younger. We don't know how these children would have reacted to Mother Jones: perhaps with respect, perhaps with admiration, perhaps with more than a little fear. Still, they would all have known that she was trying to help them. The legal age limit for workers in Pennsylvania was 13, but children younger than that worked illegally. To avoid the possibility of losing their jobs, they would only have revealed their true ages to people known to be friends.

As Mother Jones knew, small, quick fingers were required for many mill jobs, and children could perform the work better than most adults.

Mother Jones was no stranger to child labor. In 1896, when she had worked in southern textile mills, she had seen many children on the job. In some places, Mother Jones worked the night shift, side by side with very young children. Injuries and disease were common. Children coughed and shivered with bronchitis and pneumonia. Once Jones saw a child's finger snapped off by heavy machinery. In Alabama, she attended the funeral of an 11-year-old killed in a factory accident.

At times, Mother Jones had despaired of ever making things better for the factory child. There was never any shortage of children available to work. "Another little hand is ready to tie the snapped threads when a child worker dies," she wrote. She liked to say that the mill owners treated their workers worse than animals. The children were "half-fed, half-clothed, half-housed," she explained, "while the poodle dogs of their masters are petted and coddled and sleep on pillows of down." Though Mother Jones was often optimistic about creating change for workers, child labor seemed somehow different. Textile mills, she wrote in despair after leaving Alabama, might always be places where "little children worked from morning to night for bread, nothing but bread, no hope of anything better."

Now, in Philadelphia, she took up the struggle again. Mother Jones lost no time in using the striking children to her advantage. On June 17, she took some child laborers to a rally outside city hall. Many of the children had been hurt on the job. Others were in poor health. "They were stooped little things," Mother Jones recalled afterwards, "round shouldered and skinny." Several, she saw, were maimed, "some with their hands off, some with the thumb missing." She put them on display. "I held up their mutilated hands and showed them to the crowd," she wrote.

Mother Jones believed that many well-off Philadelphians had no idea what went on in the mills. If she could show them what factory work was really like, she thought they might support her struggle. The mill owners of Philadelphia, she told her audience, had become rich "on the broken bones, the quivering hearts and drooping heads of these children."

"I'VE GOT STOCK IN THESE LITTLE CHILDREN"

As Jones had expected, the mayor and other Philadelphia officials were not interested in hearing her speak. She was disappointed, however, when most local newspapers also ignored the rally. "Why don't you publish this and make comment on it?" she asked reporters. They couldn't, they told her. The mill owners held stock in their newspapers. As part owners of the papers, these wealthy men made sure their reporters didn't print anything favorable to the strike. "Well, I've got stock in these little children," Mother Jones announced, "and I'll arrange a little publicity." She called in reporters from New York City and staged another rally, larger than the first.

Years later, Mother Jones called it "the biggest gathering that ever assembled in Philadelphia." She claimed that 50,000 people showed up, though other sources questioned her numbers. No one disputed that many children were present. Small children marched, carrying signs that read "We Only Ask for Justice" and "We Want Time to Play." Strikers paraded through the business district of Philadelphia, making sure to pass by the newspaper buildings.

Most Philadelphians, and most Americans, had never been inside a textile mill to see the youngest workers. Mother Jones hoped to make all people see and understand the problem of child labor.

Mother Jones made a long speech and showed off more children who had lost hands and fingers. She complained about mill owners who profited from children's work, ministers who wouldn't speak out against child labor, and newspaper publishers who wouldn't cover the news.

As Mother Jones had hoped, some New York City newspapers picked up the story. Others soon followed. In big cities across the country, many people became aware of child labor for the first time. By itself, the rally wasn't enough. Still, it was a start. And that was all right with Mother Jones. She had yet another trick up her sleeve, and she hoped that the working children of Philadelphia would help her out.

THE MARCH BEGINS

*James Brown's children go
a-shivering in the cold,
James Brown's children young,
with work are growing old. . . .*

    —E. R. Place, "James Brown"

Mother Jones began July 7 the way she began most mornings during the Philadelphia strike, with a meeting at the Kensington union hall. But this was no ordinary meeting. Mother Jones was trying to convince the parents of several hundred striking mill children to let them leave Philadelphia with her.

Jones's plans were large, showy, and a bit vague. She hoped to march to New York City with about 400 children. She would be at the head of what she called an "army" of "crusaders." Another 400 adults would come along. That figure included the children's parents, a handful of union leaders, and any other striker would could help take care of the children.

The march had three major goals. First, Mother Jones intended to show people everywhere the evils of child labor. Disappointed that most

Philadelphians had ignored the problem ("the citizens were not moved to pity," she told a reporter), she announced that she was "going out of Philadelphia to see if there are people with human blood in their veins."

Jones's second goal was to help support the textile strikers. "If the manufacturers cannot afford to give their employees a living wage and shorter hours of work," she said, "then the system of making goods for profit is wrong." Jones hoped that the march would help publicize what was going on in Philadelphia. In particular, she expected that union members in towns the army passed through would give money to help the strikers.

And third, Mother Jones hoped to use the march to embarrass the rich businessmen of America. Wall Street in New York City was the home of many banks, banks that Mother Jones looked forward to visiting. "I am going to show Wall Street the flesh and blood from which it squeezes its wealth," she promised. Mother Jones expected the trip to end with a mass meeting at Madison Square Garden in New York City. There, she and her followers would put on a play about "the luxurious lives" of the rich capitalists. "'Mr. Capital' is to be represented in gorgeous attire," said one newspaper report, "and 'Mrs. Mill Owner' is to sit beside him covered with glass jewelry."

PLANS AND PREPARATIONS

On the morning of the seventh, Mother Jones explained her plans in public for the first time. Parents at the union hall were full of questions. Where did the army plan to sleep? What would the young crusaders eat? How long would the journey last? What about the weather? The question that seemed to bother the parents most was how the children would travel. At first, Mother Jones planned to have the children walk the whole distance, averaging about 10 miles a day. When parents weren't pleased with this plan, she changed her mind. To conserve the children's energy, she promised to let them spend some time riding in the wagons that carried the army's supplies. Alternatively, they might take trains and trolley cars from one town to the next.

Mother Jones had led protest marches before.

Mother Jones could not enlist anywhere near the 800 marchers she had planned. Still, she considered the meeting a success. After much debate, union leaders gave their approval to her plan. Between 300 and 400 mill workers, a little less than half of them under 16, enthusiastically joined the march. Many more children certainly tried to talk their reluctant parents into letting them sign up. There were probably other children who would have preferred to stay home, only to find themselves officially part of the march, signed up by their parents. All the marchers went straight home to pack for the trip. Most gathered these few meager possessions: a spoon and a tin cup for meals, a change of clothes if one was available, perhaps a blanket and a straw hat, and a pair of shoes that might be about the right size. They would need all these during the long trip ahead.

At one o'clock that afternoon, the marchers headed out of Kensington towards Torresdale Park at the edge of Philadelphia. Dozens of other strikers followed along. So did many other Philadelphians, who were attracted by the crowd. The march looked like a parade, and it was meant to. A union leader named Charles Sweeney carried a big baton with stripes of red, white, and blue. Following Sweeney came children playing fifes and drums. After this "band" came the rest of the marchers. Eight supply wagons brought up the rear of the procession. Grocery stores in Kensington had contributed bread and canned food. The wagons also carried tents, banners, and costumes for the play.

For the striking children who marched, the parade must have been great fun. Some were no doubt leaving their neighborhood for the first time. Some children were playing instruments, or pretending to play. Others waved flags or carried signs. Still others were simply enjoying stretching their legs in the bright sunshine. Very few had ever been the center of attention as they were on that day.

THE ARMY'S YOUNGEST MARCHERS

We don't know much about the children who joined this crusade. So far as we know, none kept journals, and none wrote their experiences down as part of their memoirs years afterwards. They were displayed to crowds frequently during the march, but they never gave speeches themselves. Nor did they do much talking to newspaper reporters. As a result, the names of most of the children are now lost.

We don't even know how many of the marchers were boys and how many were girls. Newspaper accounts differed widely. According to some reporters, girls made up about half of the marchers who left Philadelphia. Other reporters, however, insisted that every single child on the trip was a boy. Several witnesses said that the girls all returned to Kensington by the end of the second day. As the trip continued, some local newspapers mentioned girls as part of the army. Others didn't. After the march, even Mother Jones gave conflicting reports. We may never know the answer.

William Hartley, Catherine Hutt, and Gus Misuinas didn't go on the march. Perhaps their parents wouldn't let them. Perhaps they felt that Mother Jones's plans would never work. Perhaps they preferred to help the strike effort in other ways. Years later, however, they and other Kensington mill children were interviewed about their lives. These interviews give us a sense of what growing up as a mill worker was like.

It was a different world than most children of today are used to. The mill boys and girls mainly remember a childhood of long hours, dull work, and low pay. Some had one year of formal schooling, some two, some none at all. Gus Misuinas recalled how he had quit his job several times as a young boy, "thinking I could find something else—something better for me." But he couldn't escape from the mill. "Never had no luck," he said as an old man many years later.

Still, a few of the child laborers also spoke of good times when they were growing up. According to Catherine Hutt, boys from Kensington used to have fun skinny-dipping in the Delaware River. She also recalled picking apples and pears in a local park. Irene Brown, who would have been about nine years old at the time of the strike, remembered neighborhood games and street singers. "It was colorful in those days," she said. "A lot went on." Catherine Hutt spoke of a sense of community in Kensington, too. "Everybody washed down their front steps and swept the sidewalks," she said. "Everybody would work together. Help each other."

The children who joined Mother Jones's crusade were certainly hoping to help each other. Like William Hartley and Catherine Hutt, they had already had hard lives. Many reporters were astonished at the sight of the marching children. One described a group of boys as "little old men, with stooped shoulders and a serious expression of countenance far beyond their years." A child named Thomas McCarthy claimed to be the youngest striker on the march. He told an incredulous reporter, "I've been in the mills for over a year."

Thomas must have been very young indeed. According to John Spargo, an Englishman who helped out at the beginning of the march, a

Some of the marching mill children stop to pose for the camera. "There is no one who will step to their rescue," Mother Jones said, "unless they do it themselves."

10-year-old crusader told him proudly that she had already "worked two years and never missed a day." For their reliability and hard work, these children paid a terrible price. With characteristic overstatement, Mother Jones described a marcher named Gussie Rangnew as "a little girl from whom all the childhood had gone." A boy named Danny James, who led the procession out of Philadelphia, spoke for all the child laborers. He carried a sign that read simply "We Are Textile Workers." The contrast between the sign's message and the short, spindly boy who carried it could not have been more extreme.

The crusaders camped for the night in Torresdale Park. Mother Jones gave a speech and took a collection to send home to the strikers; she raised $76.50. Early the following morning, the marchers set out for the nearby town of Bristol. By July 10, Mother Jones hoped to be in Trenton, New Jersey. Unfortunately, the march was already running into problems.

"MOTHER JONES'S DWINDLING ARMY"

The first issue the crusaders faced was the heat. July 7 was unusually hot to begin with, and the weather only got worse. "Hottest Day of the Year," read a Trenton newspaper headline a couple of days into the march. Another newspaper ran a story called "Heat Fatal to One." The marchers tried resting during the hottest times of day. On at least a few occasions, they swam in rivers or ponds to beat the heat. Still, the weather and the constant walking wore them down. By the time the strikers reached the Delaware River opposite Trenton, several tired and sick marchers had been sent back to Philadelphia. "The long tramp has proved too much for them," one reporter explained.

A more serious problem had to do with money. While some union leaders liked the idea of the march, others felt it would take attention away from the needs of the strikers who remained in Kensington. The strike council had agreed to let Mother Jones put an army together but had not given money to help fund the march. That meant that the marchers would need to rely on the people they met for help. Under these circumstances, even 400 people seemed far too many. Many healthy crusaders were sent home almost as soon as they were out of Philadelphia. Evidently, so were the supply wagons. Though they left Kensington with the strikers, they were never mentioned again in any accounts of the march.

A third problem was that Mother Jones had not screened her army very carefully. Not every crusader had a good reason for being there. One weaver told a reporter that he would march only as far as the northern part of New Jersey. He was tired of being on strike, he said, and he hoped to find work in a New Jersey factory instead. For him, the march was just a convenient way of getting there. Three boys who joined the march without permission from their parents were sent home. Two other marchers were sent home as well—for chasing a farmer's chickens. Mother Jones ordered the rest of the marchers to be good or risk getting a one-way ticket back to Philadelphia.

Jones could not stop the steady stream of people leaving by their own choice. On July 9, a man named John Donnelly tried to take over leadership of the march. When he did not succeed, he headed back to Kensington, taking 60 marchers with him. Others left in smaller groups. In Morrisville, Pennsylvania, the man in charge of supplies announced that the march was low on food. "This was sufficient to make five big brawny fellows desert," a Trenton newspaper reported. A few members of the band held out a little longer, but fear of starvation finally got to them, too. The boy who played the bass drum complained, "I'd like to trade that drum for a good sandwich." Then he and three other hungry boys left the camp for good. By the morning of July 10, only about 50 or 60 crusaders remained.

Mother Jones tried to make light of the army's problems. "That story about desertions is all wrong," she told reporters. "We never intended that the whole four hundred should go all the way to New York, or even to Trenton." She preferred to talk about Alexander McLeese, the grocery store owner in Morrisville who volunteered to feed the marchers (though too late for the "five big brawny fellows"), or the mass meeting in Bristol that raised "a cheering sum" of money for the strikers. Even so, Mother Jones knew there were troubles. She could only hope that arriving in Trenton would somehow help solve them. Otherwise, the march would be over almost as soon as it had begun.

SPEAKING OUT AND MARCHING ON

In the chutes I graduated
instead of going to school
Remember, friends,
my parents they were poor;
When a boy left the cradle
it was always made a rule
To try and keep starvation
from the door.
— "The Old Miner's Refrain"

The marchers had good reason to think that arriving in Trenton might change their luck. Trenton was by far the biggest city they had come to since leaving Philadelphia. Trenton was also a solid union town. Many of its residents knew about the Philadelphia strike and already were on the strikers' side. Even the newspapers in Trenton were enthusiastic about Mother Jones and her army. The prolabor *Trades Union Advocate* not only urged workers to go hear Mother Jones talk; it also told them to "remember her mission and drop a coin in the hat." Another paper, the *Daily True American*, spoke proudly of the marchers who were busy "sacrificing the comforts of home for a cause."

Getting to Trenton was difficult. At the last moment, the crusaders discovered that crossing the bridge over the Delaware River meant paying a two-cent toll for each marcher. Mother Jones protested loudly but eventually agreed to pay the toll. Once safe on the other side, she complained to the press about the "unfeeling corporation" that charged people to walk across a bridge.

After arriving in Trenton, the children played and rested, while Mother Jones, Charles Sweeney, and other strike leaders visited one union hall after another. They gave speeches about the Philadelphia strike and encouraged union workers to donate money. Next, Mother Jones went to see the mayor of Trenton. She asked him for permission to hold a meeting and to "parade her army through the streets." Though the mayor was a union man, he refused to let the army march through Trenton. He told Mother Jones that antiunionists might try to hurt the strikers. Still, he allowed the army to hold a rally at Monument Park near the Delaware.

TOO POOR FOR SCHOOL

On July 10, a crowd of 5,000 people gathered at Monument Park. A local politician introduced Mother Jones, and a few union supporters made speeches. But Jones was the one the crowd had come to hear. They were not disappointed. According to one newspaper, she spoke at "a mile-a-minute gait" for two solid hours. Despite interruptions in the background—trolley cars, wagons, the "tomfoolery" of local children—Mother Jones had no trouble making herself heard. She caught everyone's attention right from the opening line of her speech. "John Rockefeller," she exclaimed, speaking of one of the country's richest men, "is a hobo and a bum."

Jones went on to describe life in the Philadelphia mills for her Trenton audience. "You don't know what slaves the textile workers are," she told the listeners. "When the day's work is over, the textile workers are even too tired to pray, and instead of an evening's recreation they must retire for the night and prepare for another day." She displayed the marching children and described their lives in particular detail. For members of the audience who wondered why the children were work-ing, Mother Jones explained the answer in one sentence: "Because the parents of the children are too poor to send them to school."

Mother Jones knew that poor children had worked for almost all of human history. Many Kensington textile workers had moved to Philadelphia from farms, where every member of the family had chores. Still, most reformers, including Mother Jones, believed there were huge differences between farmwork and mill work. Farmwork was outdoors; mill work was inside, with children breathing in air that one observer called a "soup" of tiny cotton fibers. Farmwork meant a variety of ac-tivities, from feeding animals to planting seeds; mill work meant the same repetitive activity all day long. Farmwork trained children to man-age their own farms someday; mill work trained children to do one

Parents sent their children to work in the mills for many reasons. As this cartoon from the early 1900s indicates, a few parents used their children's labor to support their own drinking habits. In his hand, the father of a working child holds a falsified certificate of age.

thing, and one thing only. And, while children on a farm were working for themselves and their own families, children in the textile mills were working to fill the pockets of the richest men in America. As far as Mother Jones was concerned, this was the worst crime of all.

Mother Jones's speech in Trenton was well received. A collection after the meeting raised about $100. The central labor union of the town pitched in $10 more. Two local hotel owners put up members of the army for free, and Mother Jones stayed with a union carpenter and his family. Several Trenton grocers donated more food. An unfriendly newspaper ran an article about Mother Jones's "defeated army," but most Trenton residents knew better. Citizens and reporters took turns praising the bravery of the mill children.

Trenton had given the crusaders the boost they needed. On the morning of July 11, the army left town, enthusiastically heading toward New York City. For most of the next two weeks, the mill children marched through towns with names like Princeton, Passaic, and Paterson; Metuchen, Rahway, and Hoboken. From time to time, a marcher left the group. A few deserted, and others were sent home to Philadelphia. Still, the numbers remained more or less the same—around 60—as new strikers occasionally arrived from Kensington to join the procession. Many New Jersey unionists wanted to sign up, too. But Mother Jones was determined to keep this an army of Philadelphia textile workers, with a couple of exceptions. In the town of Elizabeth, the army took on three new men out of several dozen who asked to join. The three newcomers were named Fleming, Hogan, and Kelley, and according to a newspaper report, they were all "good cooks."

ON THE ROAD

The crusaders quickly got into a routine that would last them across the state. They woke early and spent most of the morning traveling. Mother Jones typically went on ahead, by buggy, trolley, or train. Often she was accompanied by her closest advisers on the journey, four union men named Charles Sweeney, Edward Klingersmith, Joseph Diamond, and Emanuel Hanson. This advance guard arrived in the next town around noon and arranged for a place to speak that night. The others came in later.

Mother Jones had promised to let the children ride whenever possible, and sometimes a friendly train conductor did take them on board for free. But with no money from the strike committee back in Kensington, the children were usually forced to walk. Few roads back then had any kind of pavement at all, and when it rained the crusaders had to slog through a sea of mud. Even on beautiful days, the trip was exhausting. Newspaper reports often mentioned how tired the army looked. "Bedraggled and dusty," one reporter called the crusaders; "dirty from the long march," said another.

Similarly, the original plan had called for the strike committee to send food and other supplies from time to time. When extra supplies failed to materialize, donations became critical. Fortunately for the strikers, food was rarely a problem. Grocers who were sympathetic to the strikers donated what they could. Local union members opened their kitchens to the crusaders. Years later, Mother Jones remembered farmers coming to meet the marchers with "wagon loads of fruits and vegetables." The mill children ate whatever they were given. Once they had ice cream for breakfast. Dinner one night near Trenton was vegetable soup, which the crusaders cooked over a campfire in a big iron pot. The next morning, the marchers ate the leftovers, along with coffee and bread.

Often the army ate surprisingly well. In Princeton, a friendly hotel owner invited the marchers into his dining room. Then he told Mother Jones to order a fancy dinner for everyone—at his own expense. In Elizabeth, the children were the guests of honor at a banquet given by a county union group. All the food was either grown, made, or packaged by union labor. Mother Jones remembered a town where police had been sent to keep the marchers from coming in. After getting to know the crusaders, however, the police presented the children with what Jones called "a nice lunch rolled up in paper napkins"—prepared by the policemen's wives.

Mother Jones employed the tactic of having children march in support of a cause in other locations, as this photograph of children marching in Colorado indicates.

While several communities were anxious to keep the marchers out, many more were delighted to have them visit. The police chief of New Brunswick gave the army permission to march as soon as he was asked. In Elizabeth, two businessmen dropped by to visit Mother Jones and ended up taking her for a ride in their new automobile. Especially in northern New Jersey, union members welcomed the marchers and made themselves useful. In Newark, the labor organization did "everything in its power to make the army's stay pleasant," a local newspaper reported.

The press was helpful, too. Most newspapers admired the strikers and wished them well. A reporter for the *New Brunswick Daily Press,* for example, described Mother Jones as "the kind old mother" and "the good woman."

AFTERNOONS AND EVENINGS

Once the marchers arrived in a town, the army's musicians usually led a parade through the streets. There were usually about 10 or 11 members of the band, mostly children, and more or less evenly divided between drummers and fifers. Their purpose was to attract attention, and they certainly succeeded.

One newspaper charitably described the drumming as "energetic." Another reporter, listening to a rehearsal, complained that the musicians played "without much melody and little regard for time." Still, the sight of several worn-out boys marching and making noise usually helped publicize the strikers and their cause. Often, the other children would parade behind them, carrying signs that read "More Time to Spend at Home" or "Where Is Our Share?"

All of this led up to the day's biggest event, the mass meeting. Night after night, all the way from Trenton to Jersey City, Mother Jones spoke to crowds in union halls, in front of courthouses, and in city parks. Once she even spoke in a hotel ballroom. Not all the meetings lasted as long as the one in Trenton's Monument Park, but most did. It was a grueling schedule, especially since march leaders often gave shorter speeches to different union groups after the mass meeting was over.

Crowds for the mass meetings ranged from a few hundred to several thousand. As in Trenton, local politicians or union leaders usually introduced the marchers and then turned the proceedings over to Mother Jones. Because of her small size, Jones regularly had to stand on tables, packing boxes, or benches to see her audience. Over and over, she gave mesmerizing speeches—at least, that was the usual reaction of the reporters who heard her. She put up with applause from her listeners, but not with booing. In Newark, she told one heckler to "shut up."

Famous for her fiery oratory, Mother Jones drew crowds wherever she spoke. In West Virginia in the early 1900s, she addressed a gathering of miners and their families.

Perhaps Mother Jones's greatest skill as a speaker was the way she could tailor her speeches to fit her audience. In union towns, she focused on the textile strike and rained insults onto the mill owners, just as she had done in Trenton. But in communities where there wasn't much industry, Jones took a different tack. In Princeton, for instance, Mother Jones spoke directly across the street from Princeton University. Her speech there was meant to educate her listeners about child labor. "Here's a textbook on economics," she told the audience, pointing to a 10-year-old marcher named James Ashworth. "He gets three dollars a week and his sister who is fourteen gets six dollars. They work in a carpet factory ten hours a day while the children of the rich are getting their higher education." Again and again, Mother Jones reminded her well-off listeners that "the rich robbed these children" in order to provide luxuries for their own families.

During the mass meetings, the mill children mainly kept quiet and let the crowd see them. If any child ever spoke at one of these gatherings, we don't know about it. In a time before microphones and public address systems, it would have been hard for a small child to be heard in a large room. It is also possible that Jones was unwilling to share the spotlight with the children, preferring to use them as illustration for her own remarks. While it must have been fun at first to hear the speeches and feel the excitement of the crowd, it is likely that the children grew bored with the routine after a few days. By the time the army reached northern New Jersey, some of the children probably had Mother Jones's favorite phrases committed to memory.

AFTER THE MEETINGS

Children did have one important role after all the speeches were over. They passed through the audience collecting money to help the strikers back home in Kensington. How much money they brought in is not clear. Reporters often used vague phrases like "substantial," "quite satisfying," or "a considerable amount" to describe collections. In several places, there is no doubt that the army received plenty of money. After a meeting in Newark, for instance, Mother Jones was disappointed with a collection of $100, so she demanded more from her listeners. This time they chipped in another $50.

Paterson was another city well disposed to the crusaders. Shortly after arriving there, the marchers went door-to-door to collect money. They did very well. They were so successful, in fact, that several local residents decided to go door-to-door and say they were collecting for the army, too. They weren't. As one newspaper put it, they were "collecting money on their own behalf." Afterward, actual army members had to be issued special credentials to prove who they were.

The amounts of money donated by the residents of Paterson and Newark were unusually large. When newspapers gave specific figures, they tended to be much smaller. Even the "cheering sums" donated in some cities often turned out to be less than $75, and many meetings didn't bring in anything close to that. In at least one case, the collection netted just $3. At one point during the march, Jones announced that the army had sent $5,000 to Philadelphia to help the strike effort. Unless there were other sources of income unreported by the newspapers, this was surely wishful thinking.

Finally, after the last donation was gathered, it was time to find sleeping quarters. Getting a place for the night was a lot like getting food. The army relied heavily on the generosity of local people. Mother Jones generally stayed with union members. Once in a while a hotel owner gave her a free room for the night. The few women on the trip stayed with her whenever possible, and apparently any girls who were along did so as well. For the men and boys, though, things were a little more complicated. In Trenton and several other towns, union members took the marchers into their own homes. More often, boys stretched out blankets on the floors of union headquarters. Once, the army spent the night in an old dance hall behind a saloon.

The children also camped out several times. When the weather was nice, the crusaders enjoyed outdoor living thoroughly. One reporter, visiting a camp, described the scene as "like a picnic." Marchers "were scattered about in the grove pitching quoits [iron rings], reading newspapers, and sleeping on the grass." The children had been swimming and had washed their clothes. A "pyramid of tin cups" stood by the fire, awaiting dinner. "This outing is good for them while their strike lasts," Mother Jones said. Though one newspaper felt she was mistreating the children she brought with her, most observers disagreed. As Mother Jones pointed out, "They will never have another holiday like this."

Unfortunately, the weather was not always favorable, and sleeping indoors was not always an option. One hot and stormy night, the army reached an estate belonging to former President Grover Cleveland. Cleveland wasn't home. Luckily, a caretaker gave the crusaders permission to sleep in Cleveland's barns.

Mother Jones showed her care and concern for workers in many ways.
In this photograph, taken in Colorado, Jones helps a striker's child with
her boots.

A few nights later, some marchers did have to sleep outdoors in a pouring rain. Their blankets and tents weren't much use against the storm, and to make matters worse, they were bothered by swarms of mosquitoes. The next day, several marchers went home in disgust. "It's all right for Mother Jones," one man complained. "She sleeps in a hotel. I would rather work sixty hours a day than to endure this torture." Thereafter, Mother Jones did her best to make sure no one had to sleep outdoors in poor weather.

SPYING ON THE ARMY

While the march across New Jersey usually followed a routine, some days were more exciting than others. According to one story, for instance, Mother Jones stayed a night in a Hoboken hotel as a guest of the owner. The owner might have expected his guest to be grateful, but she wasn't. Instead, Mother Jones got to talking to the hotel workers. When they told her they were poorly treated and underpaid, Jones began to organize them into a union. Then she scheduled a strike for that very evening! She was kicked out of the hotel for her troubles.

In New Brunswick, the crusaders had several visitors, including a local man described as a "well-to-do shoe dealer." While touring the camp, this man met a 14-year-old marcher with the same name as his own, Frank Stacy. The older Frank Stacy thought that the boy looked like his dead brother, and with good reason—the younger Frank Stacy turned out to be the shoe dealer's nephew. The families had lost touch, and young Frank, now an orphan, had been a mill boy for two years. According to the *Newark Sunday News,* the elder Stacy put the younger one in his "big touring auto" and whisked him off to his "country home," planning to adopt the boy.

But the most dramatic moment in New Jersey occurred a few days later. On July 18, Mother Jones announced that she had been followed by secret agents ever since leaving Trenton. They were "from Washington," she said, and they were trying to disrupt the march. She told reporters that all the desertions had been the work of secret agents, and that the agents intended to stop the army completely at Paterson. Mother Jones also claimed that several marchers had been "approached" by the agents.

Unfortunately, Mother Jones never made it clear how she got her information. Nor did she say who had hired the agents or just how they planned to stop the march. As a result, even her supporters were skeptical. A prolabor German-language newspaper, the *New Jersey Freie Zeitung,* conceded that Jones's information might be right, but wondered, "Who in the world would take on the effort and cost of such an operation?" Secret agents or no, the march continued.

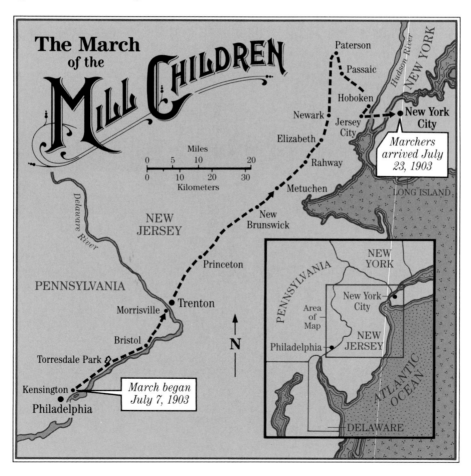

A few days later, Mother Jones brought up the issue of secret agents again. This time, she named the agency: the Secret Service, the police force in charge of protecting the president and other government officials. She accused Secret Service men of spying on her through the keyhole of her hotel room. No one knows whether Mother Jones was telling the truth, lying in order to fire up her supporters, or simply imagining things. But by the time the crusaders reached the Hudson River, the Secret Service certainly had reason to worry about Mother Jones. For, while the marchers were crossing New Jersey, Mother Jones and her army had made a major change in plan.

Opposite page: Kensington's mill children were to cross parts of three states in the course of their march.

DEAR MR. PRESIDENT

*At last I was sick in bed
for two or three days with a fever,
and when I crawled out I made up
my mind that I would rather go to
hell than to go back to that mill.*

　　—Anonymous mill worker,
employed since he was a little boy

From the start of the march, Mother Jones had intended to bring the mill children to New York City and embarrass bankers, businessmen, and other capitalists. But about a week into the trip, she had another idea. Instead of ending the march with the Mr. and Mrs. Mill Owner pageant at Madison Square Garden, she would use the children to argue for new and better laws. More specifically, she planned to bring her army to visit Theodore Roosevelt, the president of the United States.

President Roosevelt had a summer home in Oyster Bay, New York, not far east of Manhattan. All along, Mother Jones had talked vaguely of seeing Roosevelt along with the capitalists. By the time the army reached the middle of New Jersey, meeting with the president became the focus of the trip. Mother Jones hoped to ask for his help in wiping out what she called "the crime of child slavery." "I thought that President Roosevelt might see these mill children," she explained, "and compare them with his own little ones who were spending the summer on the seashore."

On July 15, Mother Jones and her advisers sent a letter to Roosevelt. Copies were sent to several newspapers as well. Jones and her advisers barely mentioned capitalists. Instead, the letter asked the president whether the army could visit him at his Oyster Bay estate. Jones also begged him to work for a law that would ban child labor, not just in the Kensington mills but across the nation.

"THE LONG GREY LINE OF LITTLE CHILDREN"

Mother Jones knew the extent of the child labor problem. In 1900, the United States Department of Labor estimated that 1,750,000 children under 16 were working around the country. Most reformers ridiculed that figure as far too low. Textile mills probably employed more American children than any other industry.

President
Theodore Roosevelt

"Their shoulders were round, their chests narrow," Mother Jones wrote of
the children who worked in coal mines. This West Virginia "tipple boy"
was photographed in 1908.

Plenty of other children worked in businesses besides textiles. In Philadelphia alone, children held nearly a hundred different kinds of jobs. They worked in department stores, they sold newspapers, and they made artificial flowers. Children worked in glass factories, bottling plants, and butcher shops. And in many cases, the work was even more dangerous, more repetitive, or more strenuous than what young textile workers faced.

Mother Jones knew firsthand what things were like for children working in coal mines. Boys as young as seven worked in what she called "the tombs of the earth," the dark, lonely world underground. "Trap boys" opened and shut doors deep inside the mines. "Breaker boys" worked in unheated buildings above ground, using their bare hands to sort coal from the rest of the rocks the miners dug up. The work could have been done by machinery, Mother Jones believed, but it wasn't. "Flesh and blood," a labor leader wrote, is cheaper than "iron and steel."

Things were not much better elsewhere. A child who worked at a cork company said the bosses refused to give out bandages for cut fingers. At a glass factory, boys hired to carry heavy trays back and forth between ovens walked or ran about 25 miles *every day*. In an Ohio town, one boy started selling newspapers at the age of two and a half. According to one activist, most newsboys were in such poor health that they were "unfitted for any occupation." A labor leader watched a six-year-old girl in New York City carry bundles of cloth up five flights of stairs to a sewing room, one bundle after another, all day long. "The mother cannot understand why the child is not well," she wrote in despair.

Perhaps the worst conditions of all were in the shrimp and oyster canning factories of the Deep South. The canners' day usually began at three in the morning. "When they don't get up by then," a factory manager said, "I go and get them up." Even the bosses of the factories agreed that the workers' constant exposure to cold salt water did terrible things to their fingers. Still, no one wore gloves; it would slow the workers down and cost money. Entire families sat or stood together around a pot, slitting oyster shells apart or cracking open shrimp. Even little children worked.

The mother of a five-year-old complained, "He kin make fifteen cents any day he wants to work, but he won't do it steady." A three-year-old's mother proudly told an investigator, "I'm learnin' her the trade." Only the very youngest stayed at home. One family left their six-month-old baby alone from four in the morning till noon, almost every single day.

CHILD LABOR LAWS

Still, the United States government had never passed a law that regulated child labor. Child labor laws were considered the business of states. Even sympathetic members of Congress often advised reformers to talk to their state legislators, believing that the Constitution let only the states pass laws regarding child workers. Unfortunately, most states hadn't done much to protect their children. By the time of the march, only a few had passed laws that were at all effective. Most of these states were in the Midwest. Pennsylvania was not among them.

The few cents this four-year-old oyster shucker in Louisiana earned each week helped her family survive.

Glass factories, such as the one where these Virginia boys worked, were unpleasant places. "It was fiery hot near the furnace," one observer wrote after a winter visit, "but icy cold a few feet off."

Even laws that looked good at first often failed to help children. In Alabama, for instance, lawmakers made it a crime to employ a child under age 14. But cotton mills and parents protested, so legislators changed the bill. Under the new law, children under 14 could still work in a handful of counties. That may not seem like a big change, but every single textile factory in the state was located in one of those counties. In effect, the new law protected almost none of Alabama's child workers.

There were similar cases around the country. A Missouri child labor law applied only to towns where at least 30,000 people lived. That was a good reason for factories to move to smaller cities, and many did. Pennsylvania once passed a law that made it illegal for children to work at night, except in the glass industry. North Carolina set a legal minimum age of 12 for workers in cotton mills, but the state said that younger children could work if their fathers were dead or disabled.

The plight of newsboys and newsgirls in New York and other large cities was particularly harsh. Up hours before dawn to collect the papers, the sellers had to stand outdoors for hours in all kinds of weather.

Many other bills never became law at all. Dozens of businesses threatened to leave states that tried to pass stricter laws. Not many legislatures were brave enough to test these threats. In 1885, so many factories threatened the New York government with moving out of state that lawmakers turned down a bill that would have raised the minimum working age to 12. Mother Jones was furious that southern states, in particular, seemed unable to pass even mild child labor bills. "Whenever a southern state attempts reform," she said, "the mill owners, who are for the most part northerners, threaten to close the mills."

MAKING LAWS STICK

But even good laws can only work with enforcement. In 1903, Pennsylvania required children to be at least 13 before they could work in textile mills. Unfortunately, getting around this law was very easy. No proof of age was required. If parents swore that a child was 13, then 13 became the child's legal age. "They told fibs in those days," remembered William Hartley, the Kensington mill boy. "It was the common thing to get the kids working." Most of the mill children who marched across New Jersey had two ages. They told their official age to their bosses; their real age was only for the union. "How old are you?" a reformer once asked a group of Pennsylvania child workers. "The answer came back in a grand chorus," he remembered: "'Thirteen!'"

Factory inspection was a similar issue. Most states hired people to investigate workplaces. Part of the job was to make certain that child labor laws were not being broken. Inspectors would enter mills and ask children for proof of their ages. If a worker turned out to be too young, the mill owner could face a fine. But only one state, Wisconsin, took inspection seriously enough to make it work. In other states, employers could break the law and be reasonably sure they would not be caught.

Part of the problem was that factory inspectors were badly overworked. When New York began inspecting factories in 1883, two inspectors had to cover the entire state. One year, Pennsylvania gave every single inspector two weeks off for Christmas—exactly when businesses

These girls, spinners in a North Carolina mill, may have been too young to be working legally. But it's doubtful that any inspector ever questioned them.

were most desperate for new workers, no matter what their age. The terrible conditions in shrimp and oyster canneries were partly due to the fact that Mississippi had only one factory inspector. He told a researcher that his job was "hopeless."

Even states with plenty of inspectors had problems. Some dishonest officials took money from factories to overlook violations. Others were personal friends of mill owners. If inspectors themselves took their jobs seriously, members of their staffs sometimes did not. Manufacturers often paid inspectors' assistants to alert them when a "surprise" visit was scheduled. That gave owners time to clear the underage children out of the building or to lock them in broom closets, as happened in at least one North Carolina factory. If an underage child was caught working, factory owners often claimed that the child wasn't a regular employee. Instead, they insisted, the child had just "wandered in." It was usually very time-consuming to prove otherwise.

Not that factory owners faced serious penalties when they did break the law. In many states, manufacturers could escape penalties if they did not know that a child worker was underage. Some business owners simply swore that they had no idea how old their workers really were, thus avoiding fines. In other states, the fines were so small that companies didn't mind paying them. Since a child might work for half an adult's wages, factories hiring children saved so much in wages that they could afford even a large fine now and then. In a famous New York court case, reformers worked around the clock to prove that a company had knowingly hired an underage girl. Their determination paid off. The company was found guilty. The reformers pleaded for a fine in the thousands of dollars. Instead, the company was charged $50.

"WE ASK YOU, MR. PRESIDENT"

Along with many other reformers, Mother Jones hoped for a national child labor law. Both houses of Congress would have to pass such a bill. The president would have to sign it. But once passed, the law would apply to every state, every county, and every town in the nation. With a national law, factories could no longer threaten to move away if a state tried to protect its children. The federal government could force states to hire inspectors, provide real education, and make parents prove their children's ages. The government could make sure there were substantial penalties attached to breaking child labor laws, whether in Missouri, Mississippi, or Massachusetts. Mother Jones knew that no one political leader working alone could change the system. But no one in the country had more power than President Roosevelt. If he wanted to help children, she decided, he could use his influence to pass a national law.

The eight-year-old in the foreground and her coworkers all needed two boxes to sit on to reach their machines in a canning factory.

Mother Jones's army had two goals. One was to convince Roosevelt that child labor was a problem. The other was to convince him that the federal government could—and must—get involved if the states would not do what was right. For the first time all trip, Mother Jones toned down her rhetoric. "We ask you, Mr. President," she wrote in her letter, "if our commercial greatness has not cost us too much by being built upon the quivering hearts of helpless children." It was a surprisingly tame statement for Mother Jones. Still, perhaps it would do the trick.

No doubt the marching children were excited at the prospect of seeing the president. But most observers felt the meeting would never take place. A Newark newspaper predicted that Mother Jones's letter to Roosevelt would be ignored altogether.

Rumors sprang up that a stone wall was being constructed around the president's estate. Several reporters suggested that the march would be broken up in New York City. As for Mother Jones, she was curiously calm about the whole thing. "We intend to go on to Oyster Bay nevertheless," she said. "If the President or people there desire to be discourteous to us, why, that is their lookout."

Mother Jones couldn't resist an occasional jab at Roosevelt. If he refused to see the children, she told a Newark reporter, perhaps it would be because "they do not work strenuously enough to suit him." But for the most part, she expressed confidence that Roosevelt would meet with the mill children. "We will approach the President as respectable people," she said, "and feel sure that we will receive civil treatment." As the army prepared to leave New Jersey for New York City, Mother Jones and the mill children awaited Roosevelt's reply.

ACROSS THE HUDSON RIVER

O God! that bread should be so dear,
And flesh and blood so cheap!
                    —Thomas Hood,
            "The Song of the Shirt"

On the morning of July 22, a New York City union member named L. D. Mayer paid a visit to the police commissioner, Major Ebstein. Mayer told Ebstein he represented the Kensington crusaders, who were still across the Hudson River in Jersey City. He asked permission for the army to march through the streets of Manhattan. Ebstein refused. "Mother Jones will be allowed to land in the city," a newspaper reported, "but the police will be instructed to arrest her if she attempts to parade her army."

No one was surprised. New York City had seen its share of protest marches. So had plenty of other cities. Many of these marches had turned ugly. Only a few years before, a man named Jacob Coxey had led unemployed union members in a march on Washington. "Coxey's Army" had picked up hooligans along with unionists. That march had ended in violence. Mother Jones had taken pains to keep out people who weren't directly involved in the Philadelphia mill strike. Still, Ebstein probably was thinking about Coxey's Army when he made his decision.

Mother Jones did not take the news lightly. She tried to figure out a way to get around Ebstein's ruling. According to some reports, she considered having the army march in single file. It was possible that single file did not meet the legal definition of a parade. She also thought that keeping the band quiet might make a difference. Some people speculated that Mother Jones would actually try to be arrested. "She will then be looked on as a martyr," wrote a reporter. Getting arrested would certainly be good publicity, especially if the army could remain completely peaceful. Expecting that the crusaders would be put in jail, Mayer and other union members raised money in advance to bail the marchers out.

In the end, Mother Jones didn't challenge Ebstein. Instead, she tried to have his decision overruled. Leaving the children with union members in New Jersey, she paid a visit to the mayor of New York City, Seth Low. "The mayor was most courteous," Mother Jones remembered, "but he said he would have to support the police commissioner." Jones told him that her army was peaceful, and that "none of them had the least idea of violating any law." Then she asked why they were not allowed to march. Low hemmed and hawed, but finally gave her a reason. The marchers, he explained, were citizens of Pennsylvania, not New York.

Seth Low,
mayor of New York City

"Oh, I think we will clear that up, Mr. Mayor," Mother Jones told him. She reminded him that Prince Henry of Germany had recently been to visit America. "It was reported, Mr. Mayor," she said, "that you and all the officials of New York . . . entertained that chap. . . . Was he a citizen of New York?"

The case of Prince Henry had come up frequently during the march. Mother Jones was furious that the federal government had spent $45,000 on feeding and protecting him while workers went on strike over a few pennies an hour. According to Mother Jones, Henry was an excellent example of what was wrong with the United States. She liked to call the prince "a piece of rotten royalty" who had eaten so much rich food, he had gotten indigestion. Now, in New York, Mayor Low had to agree that Henry was not a citizen.

Mother Jones pressed her advantage. What about a Chinese government leader who had visited New York City? she asked. "Was he a citizen of New York?"

New York City, 1906

Low answered, "No, Mother, he was not." Realizing he was beaten, Low called Ebstein and urged him to change his policy. The army got permission to march—and meet—that night and the next.

The children arrived in New York City shortly after Mother Jones's meeting with Low. They came in by ferryboat across the Hudson River, and they must have marveled at the sights. From the boat, the children would have had quite a view of the wide river, the Statue of Liberty, and the skyline of Manhattan, home even then of some of the tallest buildings in the world. Philadelphia was a big city in its own right. Still, to the mill children, the crowds and excitement of New York City must have seemed like a different world. No doubt they were also relieved to have finally reached their main destination.

CHILDREN IN IRON CAGES

The parades were well attended. Both were also peaceful, although Major Ebstein called out police reserves from 11 different stations around the city just to make sure. As usual, the band led the way. The remaining children carried signs. Many local working children followed along. According to one newspaper, "The noise they made was equal to the combined efforts of a whole regular regiment."

During both parades and meetings, the marchers held out an American flag to be filled with donations. According to a Philadelphia reporter who was on the scene the first day, "Coins poured into the flag until at last it resembled a huge bag of money." Mother Jones displayed 12-year-old Eddie Dunphy, one of the marching mill children, and then spoke briefly. Asked what she thought about visiting President Roosevelt, she replied: "I think he will see us. Why shouldn't he? We are law-abiding American citizens."

The highlight of the children's stay in New York came a few days after the meetings. Frank Bostock, the owner of a carnival, had invited the army to come visit his "wild animal show" at Coney Island. Many of the marchers had never been to a zoo before, let alone a carnival. The crusaders spent two nights at the carnival as Bostock's guests. A few of the children even told a reporter "they would be willing never to go back to the mills if they could only live with the show."

The carnival was more than just fun, however. Bostock had arranged for Mother Jones to speak there. She was a popular attraction, and the building where she gave her speech was filled well before the starting time. The stage was covered with empty animal cages left over from the last show, and Mother Jones decided not to let them go to waste. Before she began her speech, Jones put some of the young marchers inside the cages—and locked the doors. To the startled crowd, the message must have been clear. Just as the animals were prisoners of the carnival, so too were the children prisoners of the factories in which they labored.

A wealthier visitor to Coney Island poses with a member of the wild animal show.

Knowing she was speaking to a well-off crowd, Mother Jones made sure her audience understood what child labor was all about. The children in the cages behind her, she pointed out, were responsible for "weaving the carpets that . . . you walk on." She described child labor in detail, even likening it to slavery. "We are told that every American boy has the chance of being president," she said. "I tell you that these little boys in the iron cages would sell their chance any day for good square meals and a chance to play." Referring to her hoped-for meeting with Roosevelt, she promised to ask the president to "break the chains" of the boys behind her and of other young mill workers.

According to all accounts, the children stood silently throughout the speech and stared out at the crowd, looking thin and young as always. Very likely they had not been asked if they wanted to stand inside cages. They were simply told what to do. Used to following the orders of bosses in the factory, they did it without question. The boys probably enjoyed hearing the lions roar in the background, and they certainly cheered when Mother Jones told a listener who kept smirking to go home and beg his mother for "brains and a heart." But apparently no one, including Mother Jones, bothered to ask the children how it felt to be behind bars in a carnival cage.

Regardless of the children's feelings, however, the speech was a tremendous success. Indeed, the marchers' four days in New York City had worked out far better than any of them could have hoped. Only one more obstacle remained: getting to Oyster Bay.

OYSTER BAY

Early on the morning of July 27, a strange procession made its way toward the Oriental Hotel in the town of Manhattan Beach, New York. The Kensington mill children were part of the parade, carrying knapsacks and tin cups as usual. Mother Jones and her committee followed. But it was the front of the line that made people stop and stare. The leader was a large elephant, loaned to the army by Frank Bostock.

Concerned that Roosevelt would refuse to see the crusaders, Mother Jones had decided to march to the hotel to get help from a New York senator named Thomas Platt. Platt had known Roosevelt for years, and Jones hoped he could use his influence to set up a meeting for the army with the president. But Platt, who was eating breakfast in the hotel dining room, was anxious to avoid the crusaders. When he heard that the marchers were on their way, he finished his meal as quickly as possible.

Then he headed out the back door and boarded a trolley car to take him back to New York City.

The marchers arrived very soon afterward. They had been delayed by the dunes along the beach. "The children got stuck in the sand banks," Mother Jones remembered, "and I had a time cleaning the sand off the littlest ones." But Mother Jones also blamed the police for making the army late. "They had every place blockaded," she complained years later. Apparently the authorities were worried about what the crusaders might try to do next.

Though Mother Jones was disappointed not to talk to Platt, the morning wasn't a total waste. Platt's trolley hadn't pulled out by the time the marchers arrived. According to one newspaper account, the children got the elephant to sit down on the tracks for a while to delay Platt a little further. Another paper reported that the elephant actually used its trunk to throw sand into the window of the trolley and all over the senator.

Left: Senator Thomas Platt of New York
Opposite page, top: Teddy Roosevelt

The best was yet to come. Mother Jones brought the marchers into the hotel, where the band played "Hail, Hail, the Gang's All Here." According to Mother Jones, the rich men and women staying at the hotel "all got up and ran away and went upstairs." Then the marchers asked if they could be served breakfast. The tired, bedraggled children were quite a change from the dining room's usual customers. Still, the hotel steward, John O'Connor, agreed. The main course was steak and quail on toast. "The children had never had any such breakfast," Mother Jones remembered. "We had all good things." Even better, the marchers billed their meal to Senator Platt's account.

Later on that day, Mother Jones called Senator Platt at his office. He came to the phone and told her he was "too buried in business" to discuss child labor with her. The escapades of the elephant might have had something to do with his decision as well. In any case, that was that. The army would have to approach Roosevelt on its own.

While Roosevelt had not responded to the army's letter, his staff had certainly received it. His secretary told the press that Mother Jones should try to see Roosevelt at his office in Washington. "She would be received courteously," he promised. But he warned her against showing up at Roosevelt's summer house, especially with many followers. Mother Jones took part of the secretary's advice. After Platt refused to help the army, Jones gave most of the crusaders train fare home to Philadelphia. She kept only her advisers, several women, a few musicians, and three little boys. On July 29, Jones, two advisers, and the boys set out for Oyster Bay, just east of Manhattan Beach.

SAGAMORE HILL

By this time, Oyster Bay had become a very difficult place to reach. The president's bodyguards expected the army to arrive on foot. Therefore, all roads leading to Roosevelt's estate had been blocked off. Knowing this, Mother Jones came to Oyster Bay on the train. Some Secret Service agents patrolled the trains, to be sure, but they were looking for a large army of ragged children yelling slogans and carrying signs.

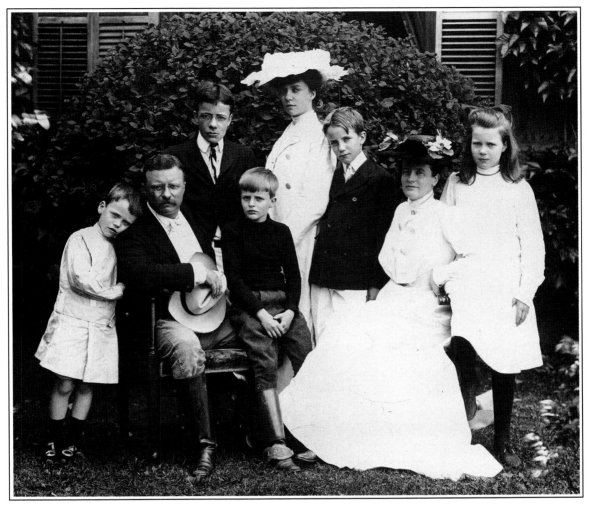

President Roosevelt and his family relax at Sagamore Hill, the family estate on Long Island.

Mother Jones had dressed the three boys in business suits—we don't know where she got them—and left the signs back in New York City. The group looked much more like a small family on an outing than strikers who had been on the road for three weeks. When the crusaders got off the train at the Oyster Bay station, no one paid any attention.

They were not stopped, in fact, until they reached the gates of Sagamore Hill, Roosevelt's home. Roosevelt's secretary, B. F. Barnes, came out to speak with them. There was no sign of Roosevelt, so Mother Jones told Barnes why they were there. First, she wanted to urge Roosevelt's support in helping child laborers. Second, according to a reporter, "she earnestly desired to exhibit the children with her to the President, in order that he might learn at first hand of the conditions under which they worked."

Barnes told her Roosevelt was not available. More than that, he said, Roosevelt "had nothing to do with such matters and could not assist her 'children' in their struggle." Finally, he suggested she should "submit her wishes in writing."

Mother Jones was surprisingly well behaved. Instead of pointing out that she had already written to the president once, she told Barnes she would do exactly that. Then she turned her group around and marched them back to the train station.

The following day, Mother Jones did write a second letter to Roosevelt. "I ask, Mr. President," she wrote, "what kind of citizen will be the child who toils twelve hours a day in an unsanitary atmosphere, stunted mentally and physically." She spoke of the three boys who had accompanied her to Oyster Bay, and she asked again if the president could find time to meet them.

> I have with [me] the three boys who have walked a hundred miles serving as living proof of what I say. You can see and talk with them, Mr. President, if you are interested. If you decide to see these children, I will bring them before you at any time you may set.

But Mother Jones must have known what the answer would be. A few days later, a letter arrived from Barnes. He stated again that the president had no authority to do anything about child labor. That, he insisted, was a problem for the states. He pointed out, too, that Roosevelt had worked for child labor legislation when he had had the chance. A few years earlier, as governor of New York, Roosevelt had worked to pass state laws protecting young workers. The bottom line was that the president could not—or would not—help the marchers.

In his letter, Barnes never mentioned the three children.

"OUR MARCH HAD DONE ITS WORK"

It's from bed to work,
and from work to bed.

          —The mother of a mill girl

On August 4, the remaining crusaders returned to Kensington. Mother Jones had talked vaguely about continuing the march. After she visited Oyster Bay, she told several reporters that she planned to take her army to Washington. In another speech along the way to New York, she had threatened to bring the mill children to towns all over the United States. But in the end, she did neither.

Despite the army's efforts, the Philadelphia strike was slowly being lost. One mill offered its employees a workweek of 58 hours and 45 minutes. It was hardly the 55 hours the workers wanted, but it was a step in the right direction. The workers at that factory went back to their jobs. "We have lost the strike," one worker observed glumly, "and that is all there is to it."

On August 11, a week after the crusaders came home, the first unions voted to give in. All over Philadelphia, mills prepared to start up once again. On August 14, members of the cloth weavers' union, one of the largest in the textile industry, admitted the strike was over. They agreed to come back to work for the full 60 hours. They also asked for a small pay raise. But as one mill owner wrote, "The Manufacturers' Committee declined to make any concessions." Beaten, the weavers did not argue. They returned to their jobs. A few of the manufacturers actually reduced the hourly wages of the weavers in order to punish them. One by one, other unions voted to go back to work. On September 15, the carpet weavers' union voted 485 to 182 to concede, and John Gay's Sons re-opened. By November, no one was left on strike.

Mother Jones returned soon afterward to her work in the coal fields, taking with her an abiding dislike of President Roosevelt. She never forgave him for refusing to meet with the mill children. Roosevelt's use of police and guards seemed to annoy Mother Jones most. "He had a lot of secret-service men watching an old woman and an army of children," she told a government panel many years later. "You fellows do elect wonderful presidents." Though Jones kept fighting for union workers, she never worked so closely with child laborers again.

Yet the march was not a failure. If nothing else, Mother Jones had opened the mill children's eyes to the rest of the world. "The children were so happy," she said years afterwards, looking back on the march. "They never had had the sunshine or the grass before, and now they were bathing in the rivers, and the people were feeding them." In fact, the march was "the finest time they ever had." From the parade in Kensington to the breakfast at the Oriental Hotel, from the trolley rides to Frank Bostock's carnival, it had been a trip to remember.

As it turned out, the march had been much more than a vacation. The crusaders had succeeded in drawing attention to child labor.

A spinner pauses during her workday at the Payne Cotton Mill, in Georgia.

"While the strike of the textile workers in Kensington was lost and the children driven back to work," Jones wrote in her autobiography, "not long afterward the Pennsylvania legislature passed a child labor law that sent thousands of children home from the mills, and kept thousands of others from entering the factory until they were fourteen years of age."

HOME FROM THE MILLS

Indeed, over the next few years, many states—including Pennsylvania, New Jersey, and New York—passed stronger laws or started enforcing the ones they had. According to one study, 43 of the 46 states passed child labor legislation between 1902 and 1909. The march did not make this happen, by any means. Still, the marchers had made reporters across the country write about child labor. And the story of the marching mill children had caused many Americans to think about child labor for the first time.

In 1904, just one year after the march, a group called the National Child Labor Committee was formed to study conditions and to fight for the rights of child workers. (Many of the images in this book were taken by Lewis Hine, a photographer working for the National Child Labor Committee.) No state had a better organized or more vocal branch than Pennsylvania. By getting Americans to learn, think, and talk about working children, the march of the mill children helped change the system.

While states began to pass laws that worked, Mother Jones's dream of a national child labor law remained just a dream. Even if the children had managed to see President Roosevelt, it is doubtful that any federal laws would have been passed. In 1906, a federal child labor bill was defeated in Congress. Echoing Roosevelt, many of the bill's opponents said they disliked child labor, but that they believed only states had the authority to make laws against it. In 1916, a bill was passed, but the Supreme Court ruled that the law was unconstitutional. The first successful national law was not passed until 1938, about 35 years after the march of the mill children.

Even without the federal government's help, however, child labor was disappearing. At the time of the march, at least one out of every 8 American children between 10 and 13 was working in a factory. By 1930, this figure was down to about one child in 50. State laws were only one reason for this change.

Higher wages for adults and more social services for the poor made it easier for families to do without their children's labor. Improved technology allowed factories to replace some of their youngest workers with machines. Gradually, schools stopped placing children in mill tracks. In communities like Kensington, high schools opened, and children who once might have worked got an education instead. Even nowadays child labor has not been completely wiped out, but things are much better than they were in 1903.

THE FATE OF THE MARCHERS

Sadly, the children who marched did not benefit from the changes that they helped bring about. The elimination of child labor came along far too slowly to help them. By the time Pennsylvania began requiring parents to provide birth certificates to prove a child's age, all but the very youngest of the marchers were too old to be affected. After the march, Gussie Rangnew, Danny James, James Ashworth, and the rest returned home to the same drudgery they had left behind. We don't know for sure, but we can guess that they—like William Hartley, Catherine Hutt, and Gus Misuinas—went on to spend most of the rest of their working lives in the mills.

Still, even for the marchers, the crusade had hardly been a waste of time. In 1903, mill boys and girls would have expected their own children to grow up in the factories just as they had. There would have been few, if any, alternatives. Instead, because of the marchers' determination, each generation since has been less likely to work during childhood and more likely to stay in school.

Perhaps most important, a boy or girl growing up in a mill community like Kensington has been more likely to have a real childhood.

These mill girls, photographed in the early 1900s, were perhaps members of the last generation of Americans to go to work so young.

The marching mill children may not have succeeded in helping themselves, but their sacrifices and their determination certainly made life better for their children and grandchildren. Years later, Mother Jones could write with satisfaction: "Our march had done its work."

SELECTED BIBLIOGRAPHY

Abbott, Grace. *The Child and the State: Selected Documents.* Chicago: University of Chicago Press, 1938.

Bremner, Robert H., ed. *Children and Youth in America: A Documentary History.* Vol. II. Cambridge, MA: Harvard University Press, 1971.

Camp, Helen. "Mother Jones and the Children's Crusade." Master's thesis, Columbia University, 1969.

Dunwell, Steve. *The Run of the Mill.* Boston: David Godine Publishers, 1978.

Fetherling, Dale. *Mother Jones the Miner's Angel: A Portrait.* Carbondale: Southern Illinois University Press, 1974.

Foner, Philip S. *American Labor Songs of the Nineteenth Century.* Urbana: University of Illinois Press, 1975.

"John Gay's Sons' Journal." Logbook, Pennsylvania Historical Society, Philadelphia.

Johnsen, Julia Emily, ed. *Child Labor.* New York: H. W. Wilson, 1926.

Jones, Mary Harris [Mother]. *The Autobiography of Mother Jones.* Edited by Mary Field Parton. 1925. Reprint. Chicago: Charles H. Kerr Publishing Company, 1990.

————. *The Correspondence of Mother Jones.* Edited by Edward M. Steel. Pittsburgh: University of Pittsburgh Press, 1985.

————. *Mother Jones Speaks: Collected Writings and Speeches.* Edited by Philip S. Foner. New York: Monad Press, 1983.

————. *The Speeches and Writings of Mother Jones.* Edited by Edward M. Steel. Pittsburgh: University of Pittsburgh Press, 1988.

McFarland, C. K. "Crusade for Child Laborers: Mother Jones and the March of the Mill Children." *Pennsylvania History* (July 1971).

One reformer said that the saddest thing he ever saw was "a little child with an old face."

McHugh, Cathy L. *Mill Family.* New York: Oxford University Press, 1988.

National Child Labor Committee. *Child Labor and the Republic.* New York: National Child Labor Committee, 1907.

Priddy, Al [Frederick Brown]. *Through the Mill: The Life of a Mill-Boy.* Boston: Pilgrim Press, 1911.

Scranton, Philip. *Figured Tapestry: Production, Markets, and Power in Philadelphia Textiles, 1885–1941.* Cambridge, England: Cambridge University Press, 1989.

Seder, Jean. *Voices of Kensington: Vanishing Mills, Vanishing Neighborhoods.* Ardmore, PA: Whitmore Publishing Company, 1982.

Spargo, John. *The Bitter Cry of the Children.* 1906. Reprint. Chicago: Quadrangle Books, 1968.

Trattner, Walter I. *Crusade for the Children: A History of the National Child Labor Committee and Child Labor Reform in America.* Chicago: Quadrangle Books, 1970.

Wood, Stephen B. *Constitutional Politics in the Progressive Era: Child Labor and the Law.* Chicago: University of Chicago Press, 1968.

INDEX

ACKNOWLEDGMENTS

Photographs and illustrations from Library of Congress: pp. 2, 6, 7, 9, 14, 26, 28, 54, 56, 57, 58, 60, 62, 65, 71, 78, 81, 83, 84, 86, 88; MG-219, Philadelphia Commercial Museum Photographic Collection, Pennsylvania State Archives, Pennsylvania Historical and Museum Commission: pp. 11, 17; The Historical Society of Pennsylvania: pp. 12, 16; Courtesy of the Grundy Library, Bristol, PA: p. 18; National Archives: p. 20; The Bettmann Archive: pp. 23, 66; Denver Public Library, Western History Collection: p. 24; Corbis-Bettmann: pp. 30, 35, 68; Archives of Labor and Urban Affairs, Wayne State University: p. 32; IPS: pp. 38, 40; Courtesy, Colorado Historical Society, Neg. #F3861: p. 43; United Mine Workers of America: p. 45; The Newberry Library: p. 48; Laura Westlund: p. 50; South Caroliniana Library, University of South Carolina: p. 52; Theodore Roosevelt Collection, Harvard College Library: pp. 53, 70, 73; UPI/Bettmann: p. 64; Brown Brothers, Sterling, PA: p. 76.

Front cover: National Archives (upper image) and MG-219, Philadelphia Commercial Museum Photographic Collection, Pennsylvania State Archives, Pennsylvania Historical and Museum Commission (lower image)
Back cover: Corbis-Bettmann

In Cincinnati, Ohio, in 1908, newsboys gather for a picnic.